AF249066

A Man Named Jennings

Written by Jannette Jauregui

Illustrated by Rick Perez

First published by Dog Ear Publishing
4011 Vincennes Rd
Indianapolis, IN 46268
www.dogearpublishing.net

ISBN: 978-1-4575-4952-6

This book is printed on acid-free paper.

Printed in the United States of America

When I was a child, I'd watch him walk alone in the dark,
wearing a trench coat, brimmed hat, with a slow stride he would march.

Afraid, I'd ask my dad "Who's that man? What's his name?"

"That's Mr. Jennings, my high school history teacher!," he'd exclaim.

But knowing his name didn't change that I was afraid.

It didn't even help to know he was a teacher by trade.

For teachers aren't scary, or at least they shouldn't be.

But when I'd see him walk at night, Mr. Jennings was still scary to me.

Many years came and went, and I never gave him a second thought.

I never even asked my dad about the lessons Mr. Jennings taught.

And then one day my dad had something in store,

for his now grown daughter who was fascinated with the war.

"Call Mr. Jennings, that's what you should do,

if you want to hear a story about what happened in World War II."

I knocked on the door, and there stood this man,

who scared me as a child, but now shook my hand.

For hours he talked about his time as an Army scout.

I learned a bit more what life in the trenches is all about.

He traveled through France and into the Battle of the Bulge

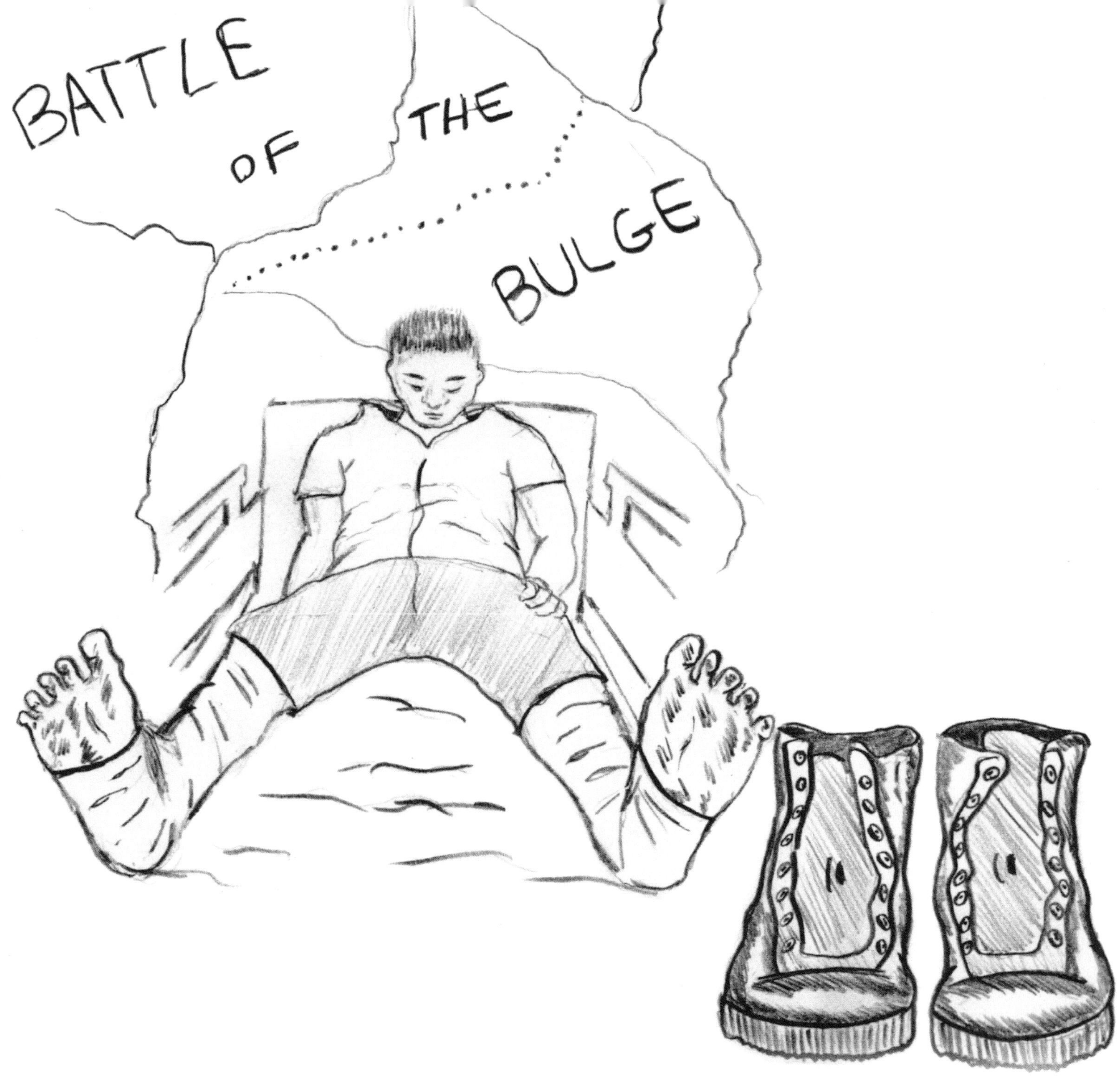

where his feet became damaged from the snow and the cold.

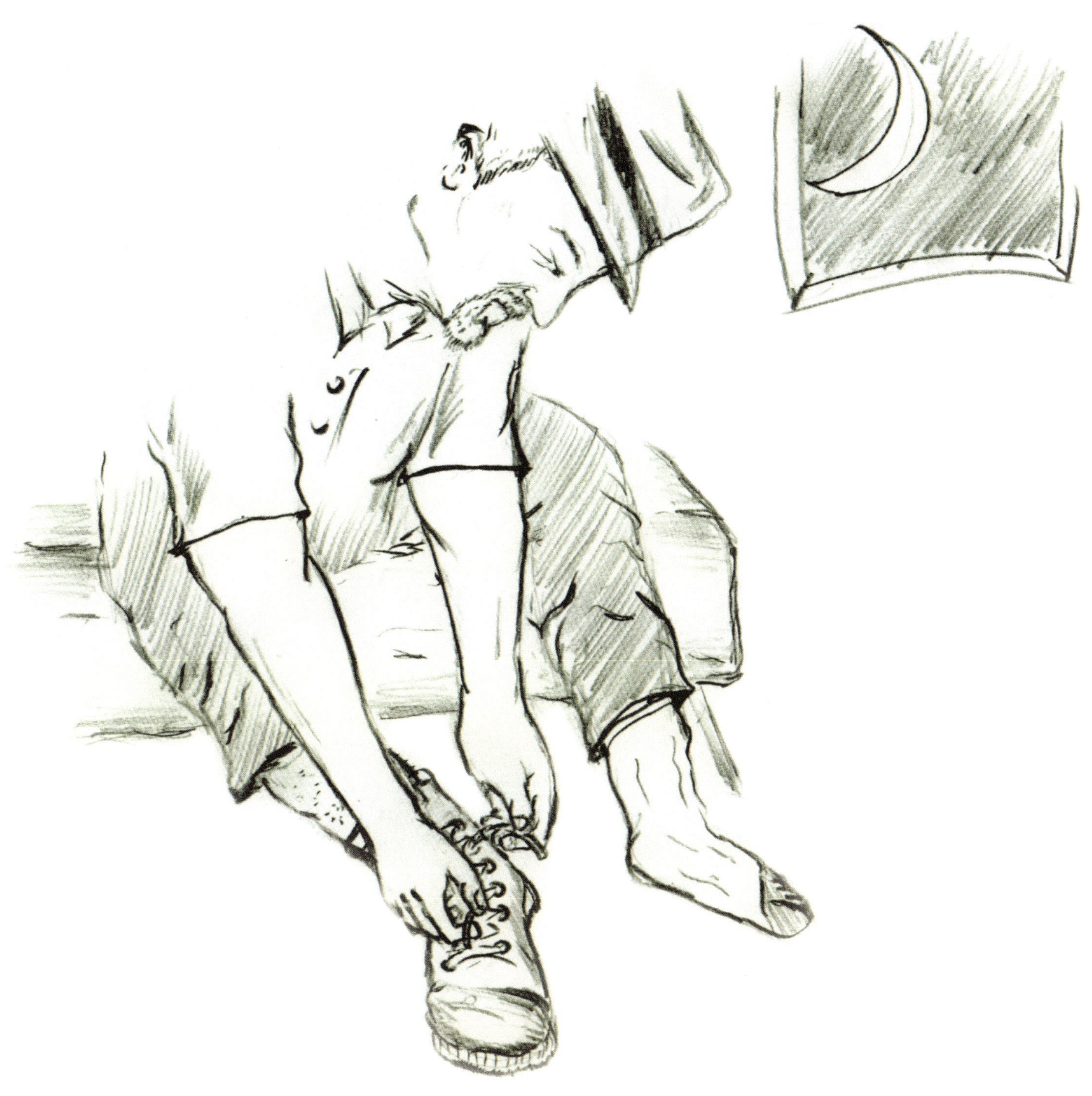

"Now I wear special shoes that protect my feet from getting hurt."

"It's not so bad," he said. "There are many stories that are worse."

But those shoes made it hard to walk in the hot sunlight,
so to help protect his feet, Mr. Jennings walked at night.

Alone in the dark, quietly and stark,

wearing a trench coat, brimmed hat,

with a slow stride I'd watch him march.

All those years I spent scared of a man I didn't know.
Mr. Jennings was his name, and he was a real life hero.

June 10, 2002

Hi Jannette,

Just a note to thank you for your excellent article concerning my military experience featured on Memorial Day.

It created a great deal of interest locally and copies sent to relatives and friends were equally well received.

I am forever in your debt for a job well done! Once again, thank you.

Sincerely,

Ron Jennings

Hometown Heroes: A Letter to my Daughter
Published in the *Santa Paula Times*
March 2, 2016
By Jannette Jauregui

Dear Elise,

I sat in the second row of pews at the United Methodist
Church on Mill Street in Santa Paula, looking up to the altar
and the table upon which there lay an American flag, an urn,
flowers, and a photo of Gordon Welsh.

I sat somewhat unsettled, nervous about the psalm I was so graciously asked to read, and
torn between wondering why I hadn't seen Gordon before he passed away, and being grateful
that my last memory of him was of seeing him smiling in the grocery store just a couple of
months before.

I sat with the image of you, me, and Gordon engraved in my head – the one I instinctively had
a fellow VFW comrade capture in November following what ended up being Gordon's last
community based Veteran's Day service. The one I have hanging in my office. The one I will
have hanging in your room.

I sat curious, wondering if you'd ever ask me about the man in that picture. About who he
was. About his story.

You won't remember him, or the day we took that picture. You won't know the sound of his
voice as he asked about you, methodically calling you by your first and middle names.

Despite the absence of those memories for you, they remain clear to me. They will be added
to our repertoire of bedtime stories.

Before Gordon's funeral came the funeral of other veterans whose stories I've shared –
veterans who have played a critical role in my life. Veterans who never second-guessed having
a young stranger – and a journalist for that matter – come into their home to ask personal
and often painful questions about a war they'd just as soon forget. You won't get to meet
those veterans. You won't have your picture taken with them standing next to you. But you
will get to know them.

When I started writing their stories, I did it for a somewhat selfish reason. Yes, I was
passionate about the generation of which they were a part. But the idea of seeing my byline
in print? That was equally exciting.

It quickly became apparent, however, that my priorities were mixed up. The first story meant
more than a byline before it was ever published. I sat listening to first-hand accounts of being
shot in the arm, the leg, of being captured as a prisoner of war.

Of starvation, trench foot, frostbite, and of witnessing a bullet hit the friend sitting no more
than two feet away.

I stood on Omaha Beach listening to a man who, as a young medic, gave his all to treat the
thousands of wounded soldiers around him as he, too, nearly bled to death.

I listened to stories from a Navy nurse slowly losing her battle with COPD. From a man in a nursing home with no family to visit him. From a retired teacher I was scared of as a child, but who turned out to be one of the kindest men I've met. From two couples - one sent against their will to an internment camp, and the other who met upon their freedom from a concentration camp. And from a man who taught me the meaning of the word Mitzvah.

I heard a couple married 70 years share the story of survival the day Pearl Harbor was bombed, and how, at 90, they still danced to the same Andrews Sisters song every year on their anniversary as if their love was new.

I watched, and continue to watch, as members of Santa Paula's Mercer-Prieto VFW Post honor their comrades with gravesite services, sometimes under the hot sun, and sometimes barely able to stand. I watch them remain dedicated to their service to our country. I watch their commitment to doing what's right.

One day you might be interested in the work I've done. If I'm lucky, you might even be proud of it. And, if I'm really fortunate, you will learn from it.

You will learn to be compassionate, knowing that with each person you meet there is a story. With each story, there is a moment of humility that allows you to appreciate all that you have, and perhaps, all that you will never have.

You will understand great fortune. Not the kind that comes from material things, but the kind that comes from the invaluable experience of meeting people who will change your life.

You will learn to be inspired – by the people you meet, by the stories they share, and, sometimes more so, by the stories they don't share.

My hope for you is curiosity – the curiosity to listen intently as I tell you about the man in that picture, and the pictures of which you are not a part. The pictures of the men and women who changed my life. Who taught me compassion. Who helped me understand great fortune. Who continue to inspire me.

The byline concerns me less today. Today I write for what the stories have become – personal histories that might have otherwise been lost, and memories that never will.

As for Gordon, I can tell you that the smile in our picture together was, in part, from seeing you. I even have a voicemail from him asking to see you again.

A portion of a hymn sung at Gordon's funeral reads as follows:

"…But other hearts in other lands are beating, with hopes and dreams as true and high as mine."

Be mindful of others – of their stories - always.

With love,
Mom

About the Author

Jannette Jauregui is a resident of Santa Paula, California. She received her bachelor's degree in communication from California Lutheran University, and her master's degree in journalism from Northwestern University's Medill School of Journalism.

Born with a passion for writing, Jannette began her professional career at 19 years old with the *Ventura County Star*. It was 2001, and she submitted a profile of a local World War II veteran. The story was accepted and published on Memorial Day of that year, and led to a continued relationship with the newspaper and a column focusing on military veterans titled *Of War and Life*.

Jannette has also spent much of her professional life in higher education, working for her alma mater, CLU, in media relations and as an adjunct professor, as well as serving as a writer and editor for the Pepperdine School of Law. In addition, Jannette tackled her goal of working in the television industry, spending a year and a half as a production assistant and associate producer for NBC's *TODAY*. Jannette is currently serving as the Public Information Officer for the Ventura County Area Agency on Aging.

A Man Named Jennings is Jannette's fourth book and second children's book, written especially for her daughters Elise and Maris. Other titles include *Ventura County Veterans: World War II to Vietnam*, *Dad's Song from Heaven*, and *Of War and Life: A Decade of Stories*.

About the Illustrator

A longtime friend of the author, Rick Perez began drawing images as an active 5-year-old. It was the only way, he says, that his mom was able to get him to stay in one place for any length of time.

The Santa Paula native says art became a therapeutic escape from a troubled childhood. Describing his younger years as lonely and having no sense of belonging, Rick says he was surrounded by a broken home and a broken environment. Art, along with boxing, served as a positive release.

Now a sergeant with the Port Hueneme Police Department in Southern California, Rick's life has taken a turn for the better. He is a married father of two sons, and volunteers much of his time in his boxing studio to help youth facing the same types of struggles he faced more than 20 years ago.

CPSIA information can be obtained at www.ICGtesting.com
Printed in the USA
BVIW12n0855031216
469120BV00005B/1